# Spirit of the US Constitution Workbook: learning about cooperation and preventing prejudice

By Michael R. Basso

I0410060

Edited by Dorothy Scarfone

# About the Author

Michael has written and co-authored a variety of children's books designed to build tolerance, respect and wellness. Michael has written more than 150 popular articles on wellness and holistic health. Dr. Basso has also written for the Yale Journal for the Humanities in Medicine as well as professional articles in Psychiatry and Neuroscience.

Michael R. Basso has significant experience as a leader in quality and reliability engineering and management in industry, as well as being a college level educator in psychology at Yale University and the University of Connecticut. His experience also includes being a consultant, researcher, and newspaper columnist. Michael is the president of the Connecticut Holistic Health Association.

Dr. Basso has a Ph.D. in professional psychology and biomedical systems, an MS in engineering science, and an MBA with a focus in executive leadership and an interdisciplinary Professional Development Diploma in pathophysiology, neural systems, and education. He also holds a BS in electrical engineering. Michael is certified in quality and reliability engineering and quality auditing, as well as variety of health related areas

# Preface – especially for parents and teachers

The United States constitution has been called many things by many people during many different times throughout history. The Constitution was adopted on September 17, 1787, by the Constitutional Convention in Philadelphia, Pennsylvania, and approved by conventions in each U.S. state in the name of "The People". The Constitution has been amended twenty-seven times; the first ten amendments are known as the Bill of Rights. At a time when our country was forming as a nation separate from our parent country, England, we needed a set of guiding rules and regulations so that we as a nation could get along in an organized way that was fair, reasonable, and responsible. The executive, legislative and judicial branches of our government were born to help make the U.S. strong. Once nine of the thirteen original colonies approved the document, it went into effect.

As a 'meeting of the minds,' conflict eventually brought about many new ideas and made the country's founders rethink many of the original ideas to make them better. In the spirit of improving on an ongoing basis – sometimes called continuous improvement, the amendments of the constitution were born and reborn in some cases.

The general ideas set forth in the constitution were designed to make U.S. citizens safe, committed and free in many ways.

These same general concepts may also be used to provide structure and accountability within the classroom. Some families have even adopted these general principles to teach their children to get along with others in reasonable and equitable ways.

In an effort to facilitate learning, a school based story based format is followed by a workbook section.

"Dad, you are an attorney and you love history and you're fair too. They did in school what you and mom did at home. They made up their own class constitution and even have officers and a court –

The class president was like the president of the United States and represented the *Executive Branch* of our little Government.

A group of kids were also assigned to be the *Legislative Branch* of our class. That group was made up of two parts; the school *Senate* in our case was chosen by the teachers, the guidance office and the Assistant principle – because they are in some ways wiser and more experienced that us kids. The Senate deals with the other classes, and the teachers, guidance department and the assistant principle - so we get it right and don't mess up."

"The other part, the class *representatives*, were elected by the kids to represent the ideas of the all the kids in our class."

"The legislature has a cool job – they make up the rules for our class and have to come up with ways to deal with those who break them."

"What kind of rules did they deal with, Zack?"

"Well, dad, they had *criminal offenses* and *misdemeanors* which were for small things.

In our class, the misdemeanors included such things as:

1) Being late without a good reason
2) Not doing your homework on time
3) Texting in class

The Felonies were stuff like:

1) Bullying other kids
2) Stealing lunches and other things
3) Playing hooky from school
4) Smoking
5) Drinking alcohol
6) Doing, selling or holding drugs

"The other fifth grade classes did the same thing, so they came up with similar rules and consequences, but some of them were different. We then came up with a *constitutional convention* so that we could discuss the rules from the other classes, which we called colonies."

"Since we live in Pennsylvania, we decided to have our convention in Philadelphia – like the real thing hundreds of years ago."

"Wow that is real, cool, son!"

"Check this out dad – since some of the 'colonies' came up with different rules, we combined some of them and made up new ones entirely."
"Give me an example."

"Ok, dad – we found that some black kids, like me, would not let white kids or Asian kids on their teams in Phys Ed. So, we came up with rules about that. The teacher said that that kind of thing in the real world could also help prevent prejudice – and that what we learn as kids help us as we get older."

"Very clever, Zack."

"There's more, dad. We came up with *amendments* and then we had the other classes/colonies vote on the new of modified rules – the teacher said that we were *ratifying* them."

"I'm impressed with you and dad!"

"Thanks, mom – me too, you are such smart parents. The teacher, Mr. Plankstein got some grief from a few kids in the beginning. It went something like this ---------

"Mr. Plankstein, why do we have to know about that boring U.S. Constitution?"

"Well, Belle, when our country was just forming we had only colonies and we had to find a way so that all the colonies would be governed the same way, so that it was fair for everyone. Now we have 50 states and it is still important that we have rules at all levels."

"We have rules for our city and for our state. All the states together are governed by federal rules that are based upon the constitution with its many changes – called amendments."

"Without rules and regulations the country would be a dangerous place for people to live – people would take advantage of others and there would be chaos."

"So the cops and judges rule, Mr. P.?"

"Not quite, Bart – they have to play by the rules too. That's one of the advantages of having them written down in a constitution that all agree to."

"Otherwise, powerful people would boss around others – that would be a dictatorship, like we learned in history last fall."

"Cops, judges, and prosecutors can be arrested too in many states. That's called having *qualified immunity* – meaning that for certain things that they do they can't be arrested and they can also have to give money to people that they hurt. That is called being *sued*."

"All that stuff is linked back to the constitution."

"Wow, that class constitution thing is making all that other stuff make sense."

"Zach, keep in mind that your class president represents the executive branch of your class. If he or she breaks certain laws, like bribery, your class can have that person tried like everyone else – it's called impeachment."

"Wow, what a weird name."

"I agree, son."

"Dad we are coming up with rules about how to fairly elect a fifth grade president and vice president, exactly when and how long their terms ends, what happens if they quit of get sick....."

"Now you are really impressing me, Zack – that Mr. Plankstein is really teaching you kids some important ideas. Just by being organized you all have a better chance of preventing problems, like conflict and prejudice."

"Mr. P is cool, dad, he also tells us how by organizing and following the rules we can help prevent bullying."

"He's right, son – it's more important to prevent problems than to punish people after the fact. Mr. P sounds like a great role model for all of you kids to follow. He sounds like a real leader."

"What's a leader, dad?"

"Well, Zack, a leader is someone that people look up to and want to follow – like Martin Luther King."

"They say Hitler was a leader too, dad. – that's what they said in school."

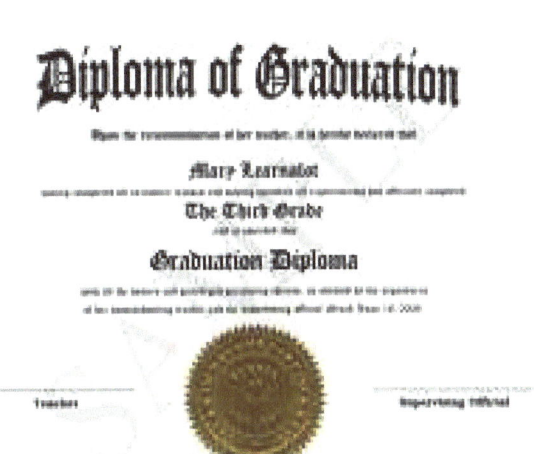

"He was a leader in a way. Lots of people followed him. – But he was sick and did real bad things. Mr. Plankstein also said that in a country like the US, things like that would not be likely to happen – because of our constitution."

"Hmmmm, that constitution does lots of good things."

"You bet, Zack. It's is one of the reasons I got a law degree. You know, I might change my career to become a legislator so that I can help make laws more fair for everyone."

"Well, dad, you spent your whole career helping those who were accused of things that they didn't do and some people who just made some mistakes. How do you deal with the folks who made mistakes and weren't dangerous to others?"

"Zach, the judge and I would have meetings and come up with *community service* as a way to have these people help others."

"Maybe we could do that in school. Hmmm, I'm on the legislative branch. Maybe we could have kids put up posters about our Bullying classes for the community or help the mothers club plant flowers round the school and other things."

"That's the idea, son."

"Mr. Plankstein, I saw Herb giving the officer in our *judicial branch* bubble gum to let him go after he left school early to play paint ball with his friends from Westville Grammar school."

"That happens in the real world too, Sarah. It's called bribery. That's one of the advantages of having several levels of government, federal, state and local, so that crooked officers, judges and others can be tried like anyone else. In your case, I think that you have to consult with an expert, like Mr. Plankstein - me."

"Ok, thanks for letting us have this constitution *for the people.* Now we can make amendments about how to deal crooked judges, prosecutors and officers in our class."

"Yes, that's the idea, Sarah. You may also want to find a way to thank all the good ones that do so much to keep us safe."

The Next day in class –

"Ok kids, today we are going to switch gears a bit and come up with a *Bill of Rights* for the whole fifth grade."

"Wow – now I'm really starting to like this, Mr. P."

"OK kids, I know this can be fun, but please calm down so we can get this done – teachers have rights too and I want to go away this weekend in peace and we still have that math quiz to get done."

# Bill of Rights for Kids and Teachers

Kids have the right to have fun during recess

Teachers have the right to report kids who break the rules of the Legislative Branch of Class government to the officers who will bring the charges to the judicial branch of government.

Kids have the right to cheer during class sports

Teachers have the right to call parents when kids are failing

Kids have the right to the pursuit happiness through playing video games during free period as long as they are quite

Teachers have the right to report kids to the assistant principle who are suspected of doing drugs

Kids have the right to tell their parents about teachers who swear in class

Teachers have the right to tell the assistant principal about kids who swear in class

"Wow, Mr. P, now the constitution is starting to make sense."

"I see what you mean kids. Everyone in class got an A on the recent U.S. Constitution exam – now I have the right to bring in ice cream to reward everyone."

"Mr. P!"

"OK, Sarah, frozen yogurt – I know the kind that is good for you and doesn't have a lot of that high fructose corn syrup and other junk. It actually tastes better anyway!"

"I'll report you to the class cops if you don't get the good stuff!"

"OK, Sarah. You got it. "

~

"Mom, I really like my class constitution. It makes me feel that kids have something in common and that we are all friends now."

"Those are some of the benefits of being part of an organized group – especially one that had rules *for the people.*"

"Thanks, mom."

"I also feel better for Karen and her friends."

"Why so, Zack."

"Well mom, some boys bother girls and I don't like it when they bother my sister and the other girls. - I just want to hit them."

"Well, Zack, you are not supposed to do that either – call the class cops and let them deal with the problem. This way it's safer for you and they have lots of cops so it's safer for them too, when they have other cops there."

"Mom, there are also some girls who think that it's funny to get the boys in trouble and beat them up too, so they call the cops on them for fun – especially their own boyfriends."

"Well, Zack – remember, you have an amendment process, so you can change the laws for that too."

"Now remember that they needed money to apply those rules and run the government – next class we are going to set up rules to tax the students to pay for our government. – Like they did in the 1700's."

"What!"

"Using fake money, silly!"

"Mr. Plankstein also said that next year the school is going to expand our student government to include political parties. He said that one party would represent the more common, down to earth kids and another would represent kids that were more professional in their ways. Not sure what he means, but sounds like a Senate and a House of Representatives kinda thing for the people."

"Zack, you are really catching on."

"Son, this reminds me of the *Jay Treaty*, led by *John Jay*, the first *Supreme Court Justice* of the United States. John Jay had lots to do with getting the original political parties to become popular. His treaty also had lots to do with bringing more money into the US by opening more trade operations with Britain. "

"That is cool, dad. Mr. P said that we were also going to learn ways to cooperate with other schools."

"By being organized and even having groups of like-minded people working together, like the democrats and republicans (started by Thomas Jefferson and James Madison), people could focus on what they like and share with others."

"The Federalist party, started by Alexander Hamilton, was geared towards business people and the original Republican party was comprised of farmers."

" In modern times, the republicans tend to be more interested in big business and the democrats tend to be geared to more down to earth people – so we must be flexible and have documents that can be changed to keep up with the times."

"Hmmm dad, we could have a school party that would appeal more to athletes, another that would appeal more to math and science kids and maybe another that would appeal more to art, drama and music kids."

"You see son, some kids like two or even three of those things so they can learn from the other 'parties' – because people tend to do a really good job at things that they like and are good at – so we can have the best of both worlds that way."

"Ok dad, so by having an overall constitution, we could have legislators that represent different views, then have groups for the other people who are not in government – now I get it!"

"Let's go the hardware store and get that flag for the front porch that we've been talking about."

"Ok, dad – you really are cool!"

"You are too, son – so is Mr. P."

"Let's go, Zack."

# Workbook Section
## You can ask for help with this part if you want to

**LET'S PARTY!** Name some benefits of having a two part legislature

1)

2)

3)

4)

5)

 Please make up a Bill of Rights for your family

1)

2)

3)

4)

5)

6)

7)

Please name five different kinds of people that have to obey the rules in Zack's class constitution - hmmmmm

1)

2)

3)

4)

5)

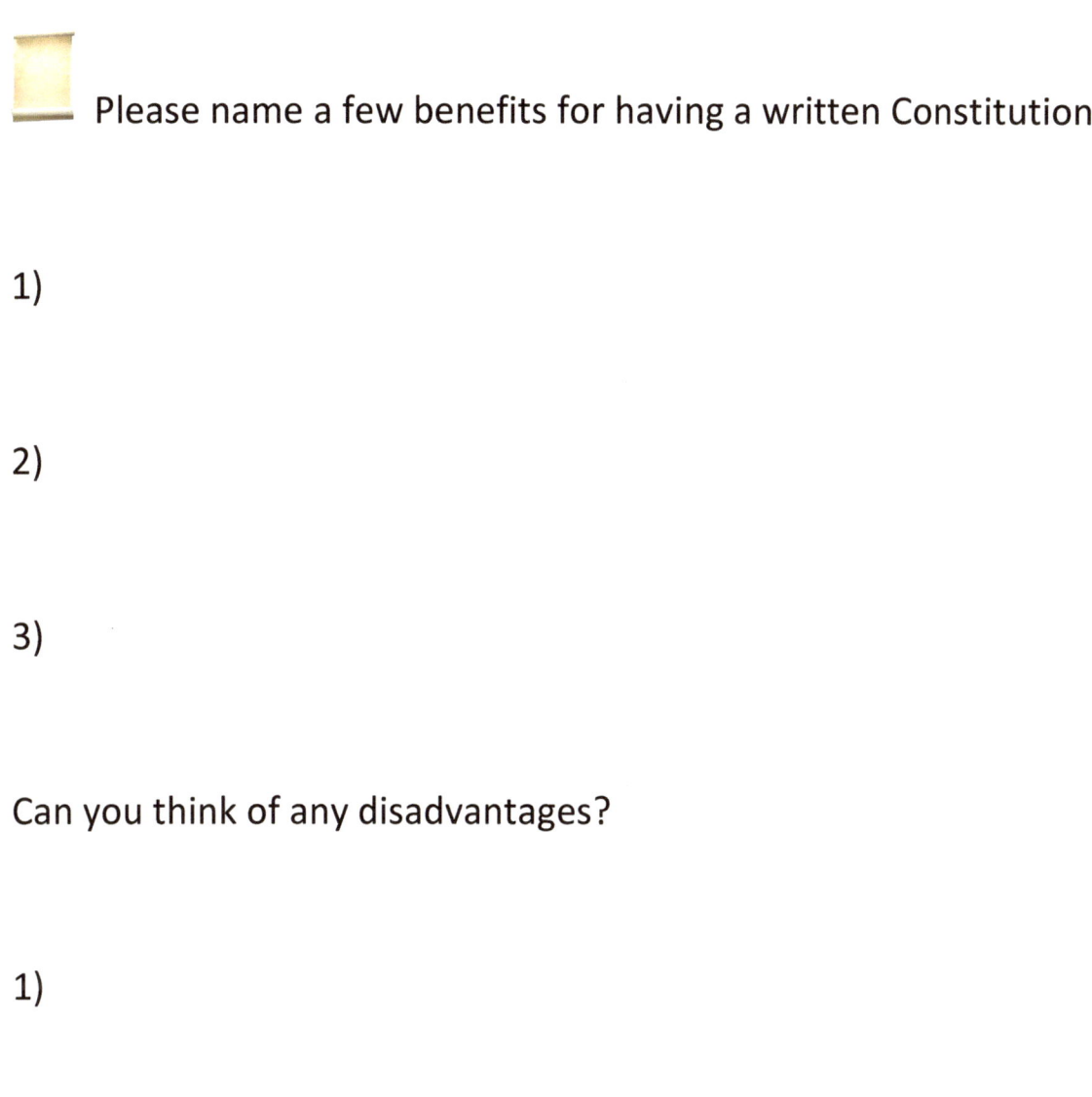 Please name a few benefits for having a written Constitution

1)

2)

3)

Can you think of any disadvantages?

1)

2)

Please name some misdemeanors that kids in your school have committed – make them up if you don't have a class constitution

1)

2)

3)

4)

5)

Please name some felonies that kid in your school have committed – make them up if you don't have a class constitution

1)

2)

3)

4)

5)

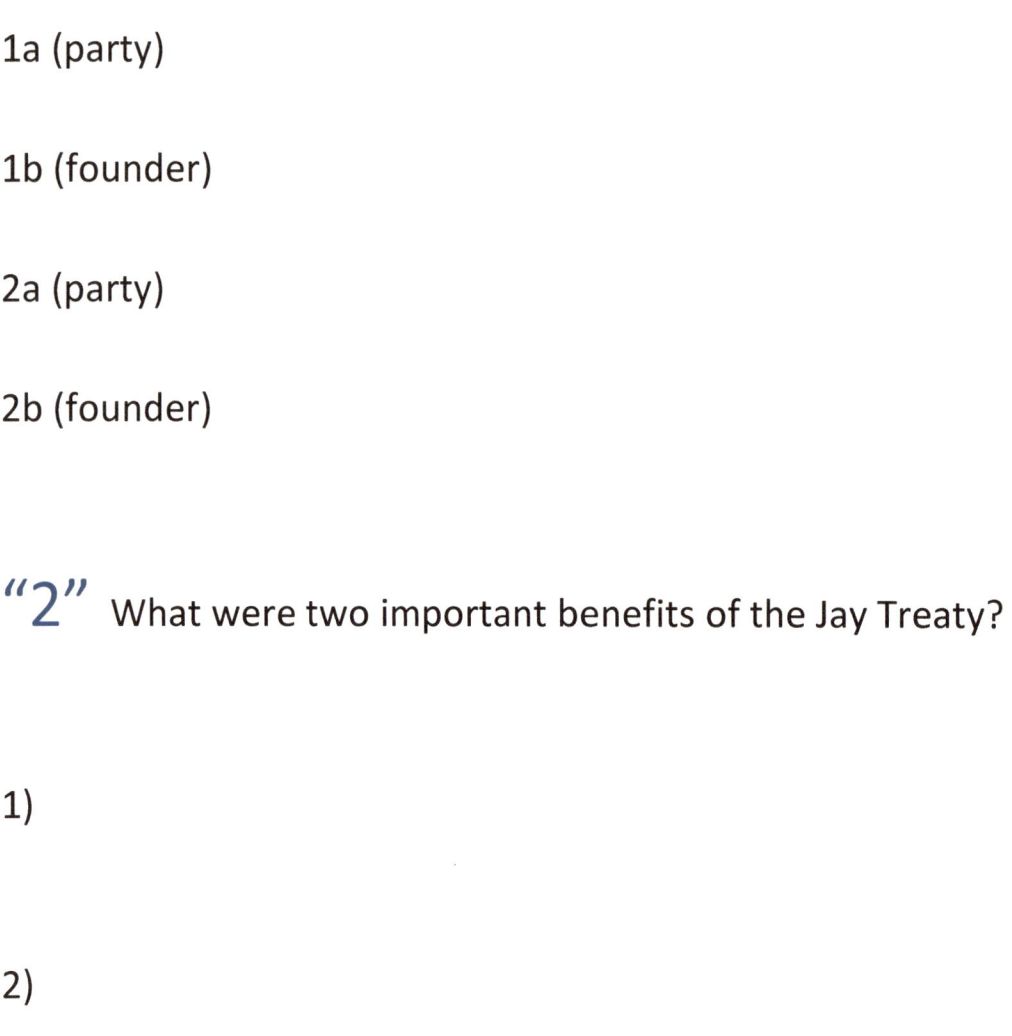 Please name two political parties that are or have been popular in the US and who founded them

1a (party)

1b (founder)

2a (party)

2b (founder)

"2" What were two important benefits of the Jay Treaty?

1)

2)

Please design two political parties for your school and/or for your family. Please use your imagination to -

1) Name your parties

2) Describe their function

3) Tell what the likely benefits might be

*

*

*

# Notes

# Notes

www.ingramcontent.com/pod-product-compliance
Lightning Source LLC
Chambersburg PA
CBHW041526280526
45792CB00004B/1397